GARFIELD

Classics

Volume Eight

MY EIGHTH CLASSIC COLLECTION
CONTAINS:

IN TUNE

THE RELUCTANT ROMEO

WITH LOVE FROM ME TO YOU

JiM DAViS

First published by Ravette Publishing 2001
Reprinted 2002, 2004

Printed and bound in Great Britain
for Ravette Publishing Limited,
Unit 3, Tristar Centre,
Star Road, Partridge Green,
West Sussex RH13 8RA
by Cox & Wyman Ltd, Reading, Berkshire

ISBN 1 84161 089 5

Garfield
In Tune

JIM DAVIS   ЯR

COME ON, GARFIELD. DAD'S GONNA TAKE US INTO TOWN TO SEE THE NEW STOPLIGHT

I'VE HAD ALL THE EXCITEMENT I CAN STAND FOR THE DAY, THANKS

© 1989 United Feature Syndicate, Inc.

AFTER THIS MORNING'S TOUR OF THE NEW INDOOR PLUMBING

JIM DAVIS   11-9

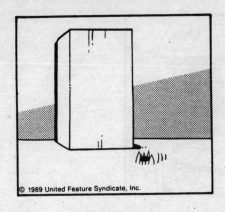

© 1989 United Feature Syndicate, Inc.

© 1989 United Feature Syndicate, Inc.

12-4

JPM DAVPS

© 1989 United Feature Syndicate, Inc.

JPM DAVPS

12-20

12-28

© 1990 United Feature Syndicate, Inc.

© 1990 United Feature Syndicate, Inc.

I HAVE HAIR IN MY EARS!

I SENSED AN IMPENDING CRISIS

1-17

© 1990 United Feature Syndicate, Inc.

HA! BEAT YOU TO IT!

© 1990 United Feature Syndicate, Inc.

UH, GARFIELD. WOULD YOU MIND TAKING YOUR CLAWS OUT OF MY HAND?

GIVE ME A GOOD REASON

JiM DAViS

IS THIS A NEW DISH, GARFIELD?

NOPE, IT'S YOUR OLD WADING POOL

© 1990 United Feature Syndicate, Inc.

© 1990 United Feature Syndicate, Inc.

JIM DAVIS   2-13

I'M BEING IGNORED

© 1990 United Feature Syndicate, Inc.

JIM DAVIS   2-20

JIM DAVIS

GAVE YOUR BEAR A BATH?

HOW'D YOU GUESS?

2-23

GULP!

2-27

© 1990 United Feature Syndicate, Inc.

© 1990 United Feature Syndicate, Inc.

IN CASE YOU DIDN'T NOTICE, I JUST CHASED A MOUSE THROUGH HERE!

© 1990 United Feature Syndicate, Inc.

BRAVO

CLAP CLAP CLAP

JIM DAVIS

3-12

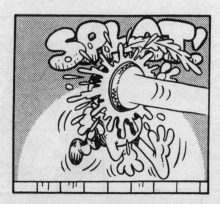

Garfield
The Reluctant Romeo

JIM DAVIS

GARFIELD, WE'RE ON A DIET. LEAVE ODIE'S FOOD ALONE!

JIM DAVIS   4-12

© 1990 United Feature Syndicate, Inc.

4-13

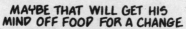

© 1990 United Feature Syndicate, Inc.

JIM DAVIS 5-7

JiM DAViS 5-12

YOU GOTTA MAKE YOUR OWN FUN

JIM DAVIS 5·14

© 1990 United Feature Syndicate, Inc.

JIM DAVIS 6-15

I AM PERSONALLY LOOKING FORWARD TO COLDER WEATHER

JIM DAVIS   6-20

© 1990 United Feature Syndicate, INC.

WAS THAT AN ECLIPSE?

JIM DAVIS 7-4

OH, IT WAS JUST GARFIELD WALKING PAST THE WINDOW

SHADDUP

THE SECRET TO CATCHING BIRDS IS PATIENCE

UH... GARFIELD

SHHH!

JIM DAVIS 7-7

© 1990 United Feature Syndicate, Inc.

JIM DAVIS 7-9

© 1990 United Feature Syndicate, Inc.

© 1990 United Feature Syndicate, Inc.

© 1990 United Feature Syndicate, Inc.

JIM DAVIS 8-8

© 1980 United Feature Syndicate, Inc.

JIM DAVIS 8-9

Garfield

With Love, From Me, To You

JIM DAVIS

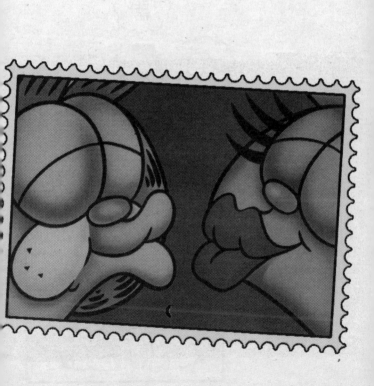

© 1990 United Feature Syndicate, Inc.

JIM DAVIS 8-23

© 1990 United Feature Syndicate, Inc.

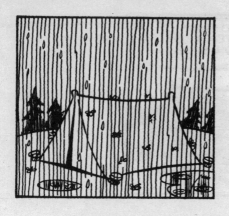

© 1990 United Feature Syndicate, Inc.

© 1990 United Feature Syndicate, Inc.

© 1990 United Feature Syndicate, Inc.

JIM DAVIS

10-5

© 1990 United Feature Syndicate, Inc.

JIM DAVIS 10-10

IS IT JUST ME? OR IS EVERYBODY IN A BAD MOOD TODAY?

JIM DAVIS 10-15

© 1990 United Feature Syndicate, Inc.

JIM DAVIS 11-1

© 1990 United Feature Syndicate, Inc.

© 1990 United Feature Syndicate, Inc.

JIM DAVIS 11-9

11-13

© 1990 United Feature Syndicate, Inc.

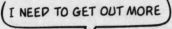

© 1990 United Feature Syndicate, Inc.

© 1990 United Feature Syndicate, Inc.

© 1990 United Feature Syndicate, Inc.

© 1990 United Feature Syndicate, Inc.

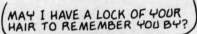

OTHER GARFIELD BOOKS AVAILABLE

Pocket Books	Price	ISBN
Below Par	£3.50	1 84161 152 2
Bon Appetit	£3.50	1 84161 038 0
Compute This!	£3.50	1 84161 194 8
Double Trouble	£3.50	1 84161 008 9
Eat My Dust	£3.50	1 84161 098 4
Fun in the Sun	£3.50	1 84161 097 6
Goooooooal!	£3.50	1 84161 037 2
Great Impressions	£3.50	1 85304 191 2
I Don't Do Perky	£3.50	1 84161 195 6
In Training	£3.50	1 85304 785 6
Light Of My Life	£3.50	1 85304 353 2
On The Right Track	£3.50	1 85304 907 7
Pop Star	£3.50	1 84161 151 4
To Eat, Or Not To Eat?	£3.50	1 85304 991 3
Wave Rebel	£3.50	1 85304 317 6
With Love From Me To You	£3.50	1 85304 392 3

new titles available February 2005

No. 49 – S.W.A.L.K.	£3.50	1 84161 225 1
No. 50 – Gotcha!	£3.50	1 84161 226 X

Theme Books		
Guide to Behaving Badly	£4.50	1 85304 892 5
Guide to Cat Napping	£4.50	1 84161 087 9
Guide to Coffee Mornings	£4.50	1 84161 086 0
Guide to Creatures Great & Small	£3.99	1 85304 998 0
Guide to Healthy Living	£3.99	1 85304 972 7
Guide to Pigging Out	£4.50	1 85304 893 3
Guide to Romance	£3.99	1 85304 894 1
Guide to Successful Living	£3.99	1 85304 973 5
Guide to The Seasons	£3.99	1 85304 999 9

new titles available Sept 2004

Entertains You	£4.50	1 84161 221 9
Slam Dunk!	£4.50	1 84161 222 7

2-in-1 Theme Books		
Easy Does It	£6.99	1 84161 191 3
Licensed to Thrill	£6.99	1 84161 192 1
Out For The Couch	£6.99	1 84161 144 1
The Gruesome Twosome	£6.99	1 84161 143 3

new titles available Sept 2004

All In Good Taste	£6.99	1 84161 209 X
Lazy Daze	£6.99	1 84161 208 1

Classics	Price	ISBN
Volume One	£5.99	1 85304 970 0
Volume Two	£5.99	1 85304 971 9
Volume Three	£5.99	1 85304 996 4
Volume Four	£5.99	1 85304 997 2
Volume Five	£5.99	1 84161 022 4
Volume Six	£5.99	1 84161 023 2
Volume Seven	£5.99	1 84161 088 7
Volume Nine	£5.99	1 84161 149 2
Volume Ten	£5.99	1 84161 150 6
Volume Eleven	£5.99	1 84161 175 1
Volume Twelve	£5.99	1 84161 176 X

new titles available Sept 2004

Volume Thirteen	£5.99	1 84161 206 5
Volume Fourteen	£5.99	1 84161 207 3

Little Books

	Price	ISBN
C-c-c-caffeine	£2.50	1 84161 183 2
Food 'n' Fitness	£2.50	1 84161 145 X
Laughs	£2.50	1 84161 146 8
Love 'n' Stuff	£2.50	1 84161 147 6
Surf 'n' Sun	£2.50	1 84161 186 7
The Office	£2.50	1 84161 184 0
Wit 'n' Wisdom	£2.50	1 84161 148 4
Zzzzzzz	£2.50	1 84161 185 9

Miscellaneous

	Price	ISBN
Garfield the Movie	£7.99	1 84161 205 7
Garfield 25 years of me!	£7.99	1 84161 173 5
Treasury 4	£10.99	1 84161 180 8
Treasury 3	£9.99	1 84161 142 5

new title now available

Treasury 5	£10.99	1 84161 198 0

All Garfield books are available at your local bookshop or from the publisher at the address below. Just tick the titles required and send the form with your payment to:-

RAVETTE PUBLISHING
Unit 3, Tristar Centre, Star Road, Partridge Green, West Sussex RH13 8RA

Prices and availability are subject to change without notice.
Please enclose a cheque or postal order made payable to **Ravette Publishing** to the value of the cover price of the book and allow the following for UK postage and packing:

60p for the first book + 30p for each additional book
except *Garfield Treasuries* when please add £3.00 per copy for p&p

Name ....

Address ....

....

....